Something Completely Nuts

poems and ramblings

by Chris Dyer

Monday Creek Publishing
Ohio USA

Printed in the United States of America

Monday Creek Publishing, Ohio, USA
mondaycreekpublishing.com

I would like to dedicate this book to two people I have never met who reviewed my first two "somethings". I will thank them for their reviews inspired me to write more, you might want to blame them! My thanks go to them for their kind words, I hope they will read all the others and enjoy them.

Dedicated to Faridah Nassozi & Jack Magnus.
Thank you

Oppression should be a word never spoken and yet it is something we hear frequently. Our forefathers fought in the most appalling conflicts to bring about not only peace but awareness that others should have unilateral rights regardless of where you live, your colour, your creed, your religion. We all hold prejudice within us but did millions die, was history wasted? In my book *Crazy*, I said it is believed that 20 million people went missing into the sex slave trade in 2012! That is worse than the wars. And that is only the tip of the human rights iceberg. Bob the Builder can fix it so surely, we can make a valiant attempt to fix it as well!

Something completely nuts

Well I am back again! As much a surprise to you as it is to me! I was sitting reading the news and seeing all that is going on and found myself suddenly opening a document and typing again. Emotions are a strange thing... they make you a little nuts. What are we doing? It seems to me that the world really has gone nuts. One country threatens another, "friendly" countries use political and financial gain to their so-called friends. Money and power have taken us over completely... nuts!

I have written in my little "*Something*" books about a few subjects and shall in this one I am sure go over old ground... but that is not as nuts as it seems. Ignorance is not bliss, it isn't something that is acceptable, ignorance in this, day and age really is nuts!

We penalise someone that steals a loaf of bread, we do not see our way forward because we do not wish to, and worst of all the people that deserve to be punished we have a psychological soft touch. Governments wear blinkers and become tunnel visioned simple because of indoctrination or party-political standpoints. Yet we employ them... we pay their wages so why are they not aware of that? The word power comes to mind. The moment you give someone a position that you cannot control (and we have remember lost the control for a period of years whatever it may be) out puffs the chest and the self-righteousness comes into play. Look at it this way a slightly nuts view but not quite as nuts as it first may seem. We have two political parties each with their own manifesto. It doesn't matter if one of the party's ideas are good, it doesn't matter if it is good for the people they represent, it doesn't matter if the other party secretly agree it is a good idea... they will do all in their power to discredit it... why because it isn't their idea... nuts! Imagine if that was taken across the board... we would still be wearing animal skins and throwing spears... maybe that wouldn't be so nuts!!!! Lol. You and I can beg to differ but it seems that they are unable to?

Okay to finish this introduction to my latest offering. I have just read another two stories one about an attempted abduction of children and another about revenge terrorism. Einstein said... "Two things are infinite: the universe and human stupidity; and I'm not sure about the universe." He was right. It is not a one off, not the exception it is becoming the norm. How do you let your child play anymore? It must be so fearful and unless we take some extremely serious action it is going to get worse... poor little people they didn't mean to do it... we need to help them! I'm sorry we need to help make it safe for our children to play again and that means we need to start making some drastic examples of the people that perpetrate these abominable crimes. (I am going to get very controversial about another subject later in this short work). Now we come to reverse or revenge terrorism, ?????????? it is my term for the terrorism that is now being carried out by individuals in response to the terrorist acts by the so called religious fanatics that are creating such appalling acts throughout the world. Two ordinary people are going out for a day and attacked with acid as they stop at a set of traffic lights, a group of people go to worship and have a car driven at them. Now I understand how emotive it is to witness the acts that we seem to see so often. But believe me you are not achieving any more than the original terrorist if you do this. You are not affecting the terrorists you are fuelling their misplaced actions. You are attacking innocents just as they are. Did you know that the Islamic terrorists have actually killed more of their own worshippers for instance than people of other religions? Doesn't that make you think that these people really don't care? Can't you see that for them this is not about religion? It is about power, self-gratification and greed. It really has nothing to do with religion. If you want to do something constructive be vigilant, be more aware and realise that the majority of people do not agree with the terrorists. It is the terrorists that need to be targeted not the innocent or we become no different than them. That would be nuts. So, terrorists, child abusers should be given no quarter, but the innocent whatever their colour, creed or religion should be given the same respect that you would expect for yourself. Or the world goes nuts!

How

How my heart weeps for the lost,

A tide of emotions sweep over me,

Drowning me in sadness and despair,

No tears shed but they are there,

A child cries, for what, no achievement,

Many die, for what, a cause?

It is for self-satisfaction, for greed,

Bring down wrath upon them,

No mercy no quarter given,

Then perhaps we will learn to live as one,

Without dread, with smiles,

With peace and harmony, with love,

War is to the enemy not the friend.

Suffering

Another shot disturbs the night,

Another life no more,

Another pool of gore upon the ground,

Another waste.

No tears from the victim,

No tears from the gun,

No justice just excuses,

No longer a hand held,

More complacency on the news,

More sympathy for the remaining,

More acceptance of the situation,

More loss to another.

Mechanics

Who am I to you?

Something less?

I may look different but I have a place,

My right to walk here,

I am no less than you,

A creature a part of the tapestry,

Take me away and the gap will be seen,

The engine grinds to a stop,

Half an engine will not work.

Take a guess

I don't see well but I can hear,

Far better than your puny ear,

Some like me, some detest,

An upside-down world is where I rest,

Legends say I might turn bad,

The fear of me might turn you mad,

All they say cannot be true,

Where I live gives you the clue.

A puzzle

I am longer than I am wide,

But wider than I am long,

I am made to fit with care,

Yet walked upon without,

I am a child sound,

Yet an adult's enterprise,

I am played with,

Yet I play an important role,

I am lucky,

I am strong.

What am I?

Gus again

Walking round I throw the ball,

He brings it back he wants some more,

His tongue is out, he's very puffed,

But he can never get enough,

I find another ball and throw,

He looks at me, he's in the know,

That isn't mine you silly man,

Now throw mine I know you can,

And so I do and off he pelts,

The look of him he might just melt,

He makes me laugh he makes me smile,

For his ball Gus goes the extra mile.

On the road

Blood from your nose does run,

It really isn't that much fun,

Now when you walked out in the night,

Did you go out for a fight?

You laughed and joked with all your friends,

Another drink you're round the bend,

You thought that you could bully now,

But chose a bull and not a cow,

One good night a wasted trip,

As in jail you soon will sit.

Whale song

The cry echoed through the blue green waters, haunting, a melodic song that held a heart rending tone, plaintive in its verse. Three thousand miles and still alone, Baboo had scoured the oceans searching for another. Her urge to re-produced, to find a mate, to find company drove her on relentlessly. She had made a dive, deeper than she had ever gone before and had the sense to turn direction in the hope that the clattering propellers that pushed the whaler after her would follow a straight line. She decided to take a right-angle course in the hope of shaking them off.

If you were a Blue Whale you would have seen the pain in her eye. She knew the sound of the propellers only too well - her calf had been taken from her and she remem-bered the brutality of it all... she still bore the head of the harpoon in her back where she had herself been targeted as she tried to save her calf. Her huge heart ached at the memory. Why did man still pursue her, what had she done to them? She was the largest creature that had ever lived on the planet and it seemed that man would not be satis-fied until he had added her to the ever-growing list of species that had once been. She stayed deep as long as she could in hope of breaching the surface after nearly two hours. She was exhausted but her relief at the lack of the propellers sound made it worthwhile. The surface was being lashed into a frenzy by the raging storm but she knew that would not stop the humans. Even though she could sense they were now a long way from her she could not afford to rest. She had to gain more distance and had to continue her search. Baboo had spent the last three years searching the oceans, singing her song in the hope of an answer and there was only silence. Her grief was too much and though she was only a mere sixty years old, she began to deteriorate, the harpoon head that jutted from her back became more painful as the days passed, she had tried to dislodge it by swimming close to shore and rubbing her side on the rocks but it only seemed to drive it deeper into her flesh, the pain had become almost unbearable. Her heart ached for company, for her lost child. She began to wonder if she was the only one and as she sank to the ocean floor, her heart failing, she saw the shadow pass by her, heard the song of a male... it was too late, perhaps he would now be the last of their kind.

Judge yourself

You have no arm and half a leg,

Yet do not moan and do not beg,

No quarter or no favour ask,

As like the rest you face your task,

You are not whole but let all see,

You are far more a man than me.

Paradise

Heart so crushed and empty,

Brain unthinking, numbed,

Legs weary as they scuff another step.

Arms empty now,

Another lonely day in paradise,

How we falter with no blow,

The strongest fall defeated,

No respite will you find but time,

Another lonely day in paradise.

Zephyr

Upon my neck a faint touch,
A warm breeze,
Rustling the leaves as she passes by,
Warming the air yet refreshing,
Silent as she caresses,
Her presence unseen, as she passes,
Zephyr.

They've gone

Another little poem, it's a poem just for you,
I took another look but where were your tattoos,
The face is there, the partial smile,
The ink though gone for just a while,
Still beautiful there is no doubt,
One look, an army could you rout.
So, when they look what do they view,
They only see a part of you,
Will they be shocked and turn away?
When they're revealed another day?
If what they see is not real,
Then falseness is the thing they feel,
What you seek you'll never find,
If little things the watcher minds,
The words are sweet they give to you,
But when arrived are not so true,
Take a hand where shall we go,
The answer you already know,
Feelings are a funny thing,
The joy the sorrow that they bring,
So now decide if what they say,
Will bring your wish to you some day.
Is it love you wish to feel?
To be eye candy is not real,
When all is past and time goes on,
Make sure that you don't get it wrong,
For what is art on skin or stage?
It's you that writes the final page.

Fear

How do I speak to ask?

Lost for words?

Fear of what rejection?

Fear of my own ego?

How then do I take a step?

If my fear has become that great?

Should I now sit alone?

Abject in solitude?

I must find steel in my back,

I must stride out,

I must once more become me.

Friends

I have friends from far off lands,

Yet they're always there to lend a hand,

A different language, different creed,

Yet each is there for other's needs,

It doesn't matter who you are,

A pauper or a movie star,

It only matters what you see,

Nuts!

I enjoy writing poetry... don't often admit to it if I am honest as the reaction one gets is quite nuts! I normally get... *"YOU? Write poetry?"* followed by an inevitable laugh and a look of derision. The strange thing is that the people who actually know me think it is great, it is those that don't that think it is "wimpy". Maybe it is, I don't know? It isn't easy as you put yourself in the firing line as you are writing from your heart, your soul, your emotions... not very macho! I am stereotyped... I have tattoos on my arms... bit nuts really because I never used to like tattoos, but then got the bug and have several now. It brought it home to me the other day when I was having a conversation with a person about natural remedies at a small party I had been invited to (doesn't happen very often) and I was dressed casually in a tee shirt. I was a bit stunned when the person said completely out of the blue when I was explaining the use of a plant... "but you have tattoos!" Although I was a little taken aback, I could not help myself and replied... "I also have degrees... how's that for tattoos?" I walked away leaving them looking rather red faced. The point is that we are nuts to stereotype someone... we even do it with books the perfect analogy. Would you be reading this book if the cover had not caught your eye? Judging a book by the cover people... nuts! We judge on what we see not what we are prepared to discover. I have a friend and like me he talks with a country accent, horse owners come from the city at the weekends and look down their noses at him yet he has forgotten more about horses than they will probably ever know. Another friend of mine is a massive guy, covered in tattoos yet is the kindest gentleman you could wish to meet, but people fear him even though he is a gentle giant. I could go on all night with examples and I know that when you think about it so can you in your own lives. It is nuts, isn't it? So next time before you stereotype try to discover. It is nuts if we don't give the chance to another whether human or otherwise that we would demand for ourselves. Otherwise we really are nuts!

Do you?

I bathe in blood,
Each time I see,
It does not colour me,
But I feel it on my skin,
I feel the hate,
I do not hate but I feel it,
I feel their despair,
I do not suffer only sympathise,
I wish for change,
But cannot find the way,
I shed a tear for mankind,
Do you?

Try

This is going to be my last attempt in this genre. It isn't that I have said all I wish to... as an old farmer once said to some holidaymakers that were watching us work with fascination. "I will show e somethin' the likes of which you will never see!" They crowded around and he made me roll up my sleeve, pointing to the top of my arm. I was as fascinated as them as I was only about eleven. "You see that mark?" he said and they all nodded, but there was in fact no mark there. He grinned and said, "That was where the boy was vaccinated with a gramophone needle... he can talk the hindleg off a Donkey!" And the really funny part was they stared even harder and then muttered their agreement. I won't repeat the words he laughed when they had gone, suffice to say he did not think much of "city folk". Any way I have decided that I will make this my last, maybe to concentrate on other genres, I'm not sure yet. Somebody said to me it must be hard to write a book... my reply... *It is a lot harder to get someone to read it!* This is not just about me or you, it is about everyone that ever tries to do something. It is not about the success, it is about the attempt. We all strive for the ultimate, to be a great painter, musician, writer, businessman. It doesn't matter what. What is important that you enjoy making the effort and appreciate the efforts of another, win or lose. You cannot fail if you have tried, failure only comes in not trying. Oh, and I have changed my mind there are more *Somethings* coming!

Hope

If I could take your pain away?

If I could solve all problems?

Would that be wonderful?

No, it would be stupidity.

How would we learn?

How would we think?

Troubles are there to teach us,

To bring us to our senses,

To give us hope for better things.

Fly

I fly yet I am not a bird,

I can take you where you wish to go,

A marvel of science... magic,

A wonder of the modern age,

So, as you sit and stare at clouds,

Be amazed, you are flying.

Writing

Today someone told me poetry was boring... so they would never read it? Bit nuts that considering you would be unable to state something was boring if you hadn't ever read it! The really nuts bit about it was the person is very well educated. Wishy, washy mush, was the description. Yet I know another that is not well educated... certainly not stupid by any stretch of the imagination... but not well educated academically and yet they appreciate poetry. It might be an acquired taste but poetry is no more than an expression of thought, a delving into the heart and soul of the writer... even amusing rhyme comes from imagination and imagination is fired by emotion. So, if you are one of the few people who will read this book, thank you. Without you there would be no poetry; who would stand on the stage in front of an empty auditorium? All writing is poetry in one form or another, it is all a matter of perspective. You as the reader must take what you will from the words of the writer... but use them to improve the mind, the heart the soul... the world.

Carpenter

I am a carpenter of words,

Forming joints of separate pieces,

I am an engineer,

Building sentences from different parts,

I am the future,

Marking time with changing paragraphs.

Words

Words are quite amazing. Words have changed the world... not just mankind but the world. they have changed how we think and act. Imagine how powerful they have proved themselves throughout history. Sadly, for both good and evil. I would like you to consider their worth. One good man stands alone and uses words and with it brought a change to the world like no other... and it was started with words not deeds. Another man uses words and millions die. The power of words - use them for the right reasons.

Arisen

From smoking embers rose a form,

Wondrous, beautiful sublime,

No Earthly creature this reborn,

Stars will bow to her, rivers will follow her,

The earth shall tremble with joy at her every step,

She is the kiss of a wave upon the shore,

She is the gentle breeze that rustles through the
trees,

She shall be immortalised in words,

She is a gift from God.

Teeth

Every morning every night,

I clean my teeth, it is in fright,

Today I clean them rather more,

I'm walking through the dentist's door,

Take a seat... I'd rather not,

How are you... let's check for rot,

Sweat upon my brow doth bead,

Ouch... for that there was no need,

In truth it really isn't bad,

To have good teeth one should be glad,

I don't know why I feel such fear,

When the needles getting near,

It doesn't hurt and that's for sure,

But fear of dentists can't be cured.

My publisher is NUTS,

she LIKES going to the dentist!!!

Old and grey

What will I be when I am old and grey?

Hang on that happened yesterday,

A beauty came and smiled at me,

Sadly, out of sympathy,

I thought that I might have a chance,

Almost asked her for a dance,

Reality hit me like a train,

Well at least I have a brain,

If I look at you, you think I'm *nuts*,

I am still attracted to your … smile.

Past

How often do we wonder of the past?

Yet fail to learn from it?

The past cannot be re-lived,

Cannot be changed or moved to tomorrow,

It is there and will always be there,

But to live it is parasitic,

To learn from it is wisdom,

I did this and you did that.

Does it matter will it alter it?

Face the past, learn from it,

Then put it where it belongs,

In the past.

The whales last song

Deep below I range and sing,

Alone and weary, so sad,

You have forced this upon me,

Your greed has no bounds,

I cry in hope but am now unique,

A leftover from a gory past,

I hear no children for there can be none,

No breech to announce a presence,

Silence, an empty sea,

Reality is coming then it will be all that are alone.

Clean your doorstep

How we have evolved! We reach the stars, explore worlds that was beyond our imagination but a short while ago. We consider populating, and I am sure we shall. What concerns me is that we have a wonderful planet ourselves and whilst I am one hundred percent behind gaining further knowledge, we should thirst for such. I am a little worried as to why? Would it not first be sensible to put our own house in order before we start looking to move into another? My Grandmother used to say… "You do not clean your neighbours house if yours is dirty… make sure your doorstep is spotless before you look at others." Perhaps a little generalised but surprisingly true. I believe that rather than spend (I have no problem with exploration as I say) billions on such, maybe, just maybe, we should think. If we took say 25% of this money worldwide and used it for research, oceanic exploration, environmentalism and in helping the less fortunate, would that not over a relatively short period of time make space exploration more viable and with a better world more feasible? An over simplified analogy for you to consider. If you have a car that is doing say 20mpg, belching out black smoke, has bald tires, steering faults… the chances are it is going to have an accident... which in turn creates huge costs with insurance, emergency services, hospitals, time lost to industry. If, however you spend a bit on the car and put it right the chances of it being in an accident are reduced dramatically. Suddenly you find that the money it would have cost is suddenly available... yes you have had to spend out but it has in the long term proved an economy. If we could "clean our own doorstep" I am sure that after a period of time we would find we can in fact go further than we have ever done before because we will have far more funding... and a clear conscience! Oh, and a much better world!

Dish

I have a peach, it is not good, the peach has gone
quite bad,
I really want to take a bite, it's driving me quite
mad,
I pick it up and bring it close, temptation is too
much,
I place my teeth upon it and they close until they
touch,
The taste is just so awful, I think I might throw up,
I look upon the table and then spit it in a cup,
It teaches me a lesson, a wasteful fool I've been,
How many other people have played the same old
scene,
Take what you need in future and not just what
you wish,
Remember all the people that have nothing in their
dish.

Waves and woman

Waves kiss the shore in everlasting love,
Their caress strong and yet gentle,
No anger from her today she washes over you in
ecstasy.
Her smile benevolent her touch tender,
A constant lover, now tempestuous, unpredictable,
Peaceful and frightening, kind and cruel,
Beautiful in all her forms,
Always a woman.

Rehearsal

When all around is now turned grey,

When sunset brings an end to day,

When life is tired and all is fear,

Step back and look it will be clear,

No dress rehearsal is this stage,

No encore even for a sage,

Be sure to live and smile,

Try to go the extra mile,

When the curtain starts to fall,

When it comes, the final call,

Make certain that it was well done,

You'll never get another one.

What is?

What is love?

A burning desire,

Elation, delight, despair,

Darkness, loneliness, light.

Warmth, comfort, security,

That is love.

The truth

We as men puff out our chest and become all macho... and actually look down upon those that are "in touch with their feminine side". I haven't got a feminine side I am all man... bunkum. Apart from the obvious curvy difference, the hair, the smile, the eyes, the beauty... sorry got carried away there, the truth is the only difference is one tiny little chromosome. The difference as a percentage is only about 1.8% which makes us extremely similar not just as a species but in gender! So, the next time you are trying to tell a woman what a great hunter-gatherer you are, remember less than 2% and it would be you that was buying the dress!

Karma

Do I now fulfil your need?
As I lie on the floor and bleed,
Are you proud do you feel good?
I really don't think that you should,
When you awake will you recall?
How big a distance that you fall,
Now find excuse ease your guilt?
The life you took can't be rebuilt,
Will you now think before you act?
Remember Karma gets you back.

Divorce

I tap the keys the words then form,

Another story might be born,

I am a prisoner it seems,

Of charger, keyboard and a screen,

I sit before her every day,

Staring in my boring way,

She knows she has me, doesn't care,

I take her with me everywhere,

I did once think I would divorce,

Then looked at her and felt remorse,

So here I sit my Dell on lap,

And on her keys still I tap.

Squirrel

I am a little tree rat a squirrel is my name,

I hide my nuts all over and for that I have earned fame,

I am actually quite clever and find a way to food,

I am not being greedy I want to feed my brood,

In winter I will sleep a lot but wake to find my stash,

Its hidden in the frozen ground and ice I'll have to bash,

Spring soon comes and then I'll be busy once again,

Running round your garden like a tiny fluffy train,

I am a little tree rat a squirrel is my name,

I hide my nuts all over and for that I have earned fame.

Eyes

What would you see through my eyes?

Greener grass and bluer skies?

Would you see the harm, see the good?

Plant a forest tend a wood?

Would you look and see?

That life is you and life is me?

Take only things you really need?

See yourself and end your greed?

I wonder what if it could be?

That through my eyes you now do see.

Get me

Get me this and get me that,

I can't quite manage so kick the cat,

Bring me food and bring me drink,

Give me a wash so I don't stink,

Slave for me for I am man,

I don't want that... another can,

The baseball bat is by the door,

One good crack he's on the floor,

When he awakes no more demands,

From asking you he now is banned,

His legs now work and very quick,

And all because of one good stick!

I should explain this little rhyme as it is very tongue in cheek. I am not advocating violence in any form! It was just that I was talking to someone whose wife had a baby the night before and he was sitting in a chair saying how proud he was and getting his other son to go and ask his wife to bring him stuff rather than get out of the chair himself. It wasn't that he is lazy it was more that he expected it... 1.8% different! The baseball bat is a metaphor by the way. Lol.

Dark

It's getting dark but you can't see,

Just what the darkness means to me,

I do not fear the lack of sight,

That comes to us with every night,

the loneliness is what I feel,

Without the sun becomes so real,

To lie alone no comfort left,

An empty heart and so bereft.

And so the light switch comes to play,

The passing of another day.

Washing

No rock on which to bash my clothes,

How will I clean them heaven knows?

Wait what is this I now espy?

Out of the corner of my eye,

It's sitting there like it knows best,

Stick them in here I'll do the rest,

I'll make sure they come out clean,

The whitest that you've ever seen,

Just switch me on and then sit back,

All you do then is ... relax!

Greener

A world of dreams,

Impossible to reach, we see in hope,

A life we cannot touch or hold,

Taunted by its beauty,

Always looking, always searching,

An endless circle,

Starting where we finish,

No respite, no succour,

The other man's grass.

Belief

How foolish are we?

Striving always for youth,

Looking for the elusive,

Seeing a reality that does not exist,

Fooling ourselves with our own stupidity,

What is worse, we believe it.

Food

I just ate lasagna, it tasted very nice,
I think I'll have another one and get the feeling twice,
That is weird I munched it but it didn't taste as good,
Never mind I ate it and now to start on pud,
Apple pie and cream a little custard on the top,
I'm feeling rather bloated, I think I'm going to pop,
My greed has overcome me and now it's time to pay,
I'm feeling rather queasy I'm afraid I have to say,
I have to double over as my tum begins to ache,
And discover it's much better a little to partake,
So, when next I find I'm hungry I'll not be such a pig,
The little plate is better the others far too big!

I am

Am I.

Am I who I wish to be?

Am I?

Am I kind and helpful, caring?

Am I?

Am I thoughtful, generous?

Am I?

Am I good, intelligent, loving?

Am I?

Am I foolish, vain, self-righteous?

Am I?

I am.

Pen

The pen feels good, a wonder,

As it leaves its trail across the page,

It wasn't all that long ago the pen was all the rage,

Sadly, though no longer, we never seem to write,

It's all done on computer, electricity and light,

I know it is much better but the thing that worries me,

What if there's a worldwide crash… then where will we be?

Parts

So many parts each in its place,

For eons nothing changes,

Yet in one blink of time,

We strip the parts for scrap,

Not thinking how the wheels will turn,

Another year another ten?

How many parts will be left?

Will she then turn when we have taken

everything?

Yes! But we will not.

How sad

How sad it is that you use others,

How sad that such a beautiful face is made ugly,

How sad that you become a siren using your
sexuality,

How sad, bringing the sailor to his doom upon the
rocks,

How sad to misuse such a gift,

How sad to find you so empty,

How sad that the rise from the ashes is foregone.

How sad it seems it hurts me more than you.

Priorities

I write this as I think it… there is no plan to my writing as you have more than likely gathered. There is no plan to my life if I am honest! I have always been a little fickle and impetuous. I probably delete as much as I write! I know that some of my "stuff" is controversial and opinionated, maybe even a bit disturbing…could be the name of another in the series…*Something Completely Disturbing*? See impetuosity, said I wasn't going to do another… don't worry more than likely I won't! I do though have a strong belief that we should look further than our own noses and at least make, even if it is a miniscule effort to make the world a better place for the children that in truth are yours. Life is not a dress rehearsal, it comes and it goes, there is no long run of the play, just a one-off show. I had to have a checkup the other day (fortunately all is well) and I was treating it in my fickle and rather blasé way. A friend of mine became really angry with me and said… "I know you are tough but you're not bloody invincible now go and get yourself checked out!" not only did I think the concern very sweet but there was something very profound there. We do think we are invincible but in all honesty, we are not. So, as you sit in your office or whatever it is you do remember that if it is not affecting others and you are just doing that bit extra to impress the boss (which it probably doesn't as he most likely thinks you are just creeping) go home and hug your wife and kids, your lover whoever is in your life. Get the priorities right they should always be number one. When the curtain falls forget the encores! I am no less a hypocrite than you,

Caw

I caw at you I am a crow,

It is the only thing I know,

You think that I cannot be good,

The worst bird perching in the wood,

But if you learn you'd be surprised,

I'm like a natural pesticide,

I do all this with my great beak,

As bugs within the soil I seek,

You see it is part of the plan,

We are not all bad we help you man.

Bug

All I am is one small bug,

Sitting here upon the rug,

Please don't squash me that's a pain,

I only came in from the rain,

Pick me up I beg of you,

No don't bash me with your shoe,

Thank you put me out the door,

I'll never bother you no more!

Elemental

Fire surrounds you seers the flesh,

Water washes over you, cooling,

Wind blows through your hair refreshing,

Feelings create darkness and light,

Stress and anxiety causes your brow to furrow,

A face generates butterflies, stars before your

eyes,

Life is elemental, is love.

I, we

I am alone, I am at peace,

I am tired, I am creased,

I am forgotten, I am forlorn,

I am awoken, I am reborn,

I am intrigued, I am confused,

I am awake, I am defused,

I am so weary, I am now blind,

We are unworthy we are unkind.

One hand, two steps

I am tearful, I am joyous,

A helping hand given,

I am angry, I am sad,

No hand offered,

I am happy, I am fulfilled,

One small gesture,

I am ashamed, I am forlorn,

Two steps pass by.

Ideology

I do not know if I am ashamed or happy this evening! I watched a video on YouTube, in truth I did not mean to watch it. I was watching a music clip and it ended, it was followed by a video that was titled *It Will Restore Your Faith in Human Nature* and I let it run.

I have not cried for many years. When my parents died I did not cry, I was the strong one. When others cry upon my shoulder, I do not cry, I am the strong one. Some say I am cold but I do not think so, far from it. Maybe it is a macho thing, I do not know and there are times when I would have wished to cry but did not. It seems to be the one emotion I control. As I watched this video tears ran down my cheeks! Children helping other children, showing compassion and care for those not as fortunate as them, amazing acts of compassion by ordinary people, emergency service personnel, people risking themselves to help an animal in distress. You know I am not ashamed, it was an amazing and uplifting thing to see. And the cost was only time or a few pence. But mainly the cost was a generous and understanding spirit. I intend this to be my last work of this nature, I shall still write but most likely it will be in other genres. So, I will tell you a small thing that at one time I would not have admitted. I am a sort of scientist and have always believed and still do in evolution and science. I lived in Africa, which you will know if you have read my other books. Whilst there I had a very bad experience. I had to have an appendix removed, the surgeon was very good, the anesthetist not so good as I woke up in the middle of the operation. They did me okay though and they don't have the facilities that we have in the "Western" world. Obviously, I survived it as I am still writing! The pain afterwards went on for weeks and was worse than the appendix, they tried just about everything to ease it and even the strongest painkillers had no effect. Now I am not a zealot, nor am I self-righteous. I had no faith or for that matter, belief in some higher being at all. The pain was so bad it kept me awake and I would literally curl up in a ball. I could not eat, in fact I could do very little except keep my knees to my chest. After about three weeks of this I was lying in bed and the pain seemed to get worse. In desperation, I actually said... *God I know I have not been a religious man, in fact I have been the opposite but if you are there please take this pain away.* Now you are probably all going, yeah here we go... I am not preaching, every-man has a right to believe in what they wish. What I can tell you is that for the first time in three weeks I went straight to sleep and when I woke in the morning I was pain free, and have been since! All I am saying to you is that we are children, we do not have sufficient comprehension to understand all things. But you know I don't have to because no one has indoctrinated me or brainwashed me but I am telling you that there is a higher plain we call it God (and I am not being insulting by saying it but would be arrogant to say him or her). There are just some things that I believe we can never prove or disprove. I can tell you for sure that if you ask and you are genuine whatever name we give, and I will say God, it helps. I do not tell people of this in fact. I don't go to church or read the Bible or any other religious book, my belief is my own and I keep it inside. The ideology of Christianity I think is wonderful yet as all religions are misused by man. This is now going to get contentious but I will not apologise for that. We harp on about God, and in honesty God is God surely, it doesn't matter what the given name is, it is still the same God... everybody keeps saying there is only one, do they not? Man has over the years re-written and translated religious works so many times and remember it was written by men in the first place and if I asked ten different people to write a version of the same passage from the Bible, or any religious work, I would receive ten different texts because each would be opinionated. Not because the writers want to alter the meaning but because it would be their own interpretation. We also become so exclusive, your neighbour doesn't believe the same as you so either they are the devil incarnate or there is a concerted effort to "convert" them to the same opinion as you... *mmm* think about it. I know Christians are not going down that route, though there have been isolated incidents of reprisals, but isn't that what people like ISIS are using as an excuse? As an Englishman I have little time for listening to those that say Henry V111 was a great King. I do not think he was personally, I think he was a despot. He even changed the Bible to suit his own ends, and that is the Bible that forms the base of modern Protestantism. See what I mean about opinion? So, what I am trying to say is Christianity is based on love, compassion and understanding... Jesus loved to tell the story of a man he revered, the good Samaritan... he understood that there is good and bad in all people regardless of their religion. So before you lay your head upon the pillow, consider this... whether you are white, black, red, yellow, blue or green are we not all God's children, whatever you choose to call it? Oh, and remember that counts just the same for non-believers! Sorry, can't shut up now! One more thing... the wars, the suffering the inhumanity to all creatures, human or otherwise cannot be excused under a religious banner. Again, we should learn from history not keep reliving it!

No apologies

I shall not make any apologies for this, though it is a subject I have touched on before. We seem to hide from this, perhaps it is so repugnant to us that we do not wish to face the truth?

Any form of slavery is appalling let me say, we still scream of the disgraceful enslavement of people that happened in our history, yet barely raise a whisper about slavery today. Yes, it does happen and on a far greater scale. There are millions yes millions, not thousands or even tens of thousands but millions of people forced into slavery every year... and it is mainly the sex slave so called industry. How can we allow this? Millions? If there is an international disaster where ten thousand people are lost we throw our hands in the air and every news channel runs it for weeks, if there was a war where fifty thousand people were killed it would be written in history. Yet right here right now millions, no exaggeration this, yes millions are taken into sex slavery every year and we are completely blasé! Do we not value the children and the women of the world? Yes, there are males taken into this appalling activity but women and children are the main sufferers. I do therefore have a question I would like to ask you. When will it stop? More importantly when will we make enough noise to stop it? We have politicians telling us we need to build walls, stop being a part of the world and be individuals, build bigger weapons, they need to drive bigger cars, spend millions on hosting parties for visiting dignitaries, waste billions on ridiculous projects and yet we can't put something like this right? Do not have the funding? I would love to know the costs of just drinks that the western governments spend over a year, I bet we would all have a shock... and enough funding to do something serious. There is so much waste and so much wrong and I am quite certain I am not the only one that sees or feels this. I sadly do not have the power to change things, or do I? I do have a voice and shall keep using it for as long as I have breath, I am a nobody but that should not stop me from voicing injustice and trying to convince others to voice opinion against the disgraceful deeds we inflict upon not only the world but ourselves. I ask you to do the same to be aware of how we can make a difference. Not for us for we are already history but for the children that have yet to come. When I was in Africa a man said to me. "Chris, we live in a Global village, what a pity we have yet to realise it." That is profound.

Look it doesn't matter who you are, just like me you will have made mistakes errors of judgement but we are still able to make change. Change only comes though with help it cannot happen on its own in such cases. So please I ask you when you are tucking your child in at night or reading them a story spare a thought for those that are forced into being slaves, abused, degraded, badger your representative by phone or letter. Do not allow them to sweep this under the carpet. Stand up and be heard.

I do go on a bit...

Okay one small one! the other man's grass is always greener... well it seems so. I did the lottery but didn't win... somebody did. In that respect his grass is definitely greener than mine! On the whole though the grass is just the same, we are the ones that make the other man's grass greener because apart from the lottery winner who at this moment is probably far too ecstatic to even think about grass! You see your neighbour's wife walking down the street in her high heel shoes tanned legs... I'll stop there... and you are drooling... your neighbour probably does the same thing when he sees your wife! Familiarity breeds contempt for one thing and even if your neighbour's wife looks like she has just stepped off the catwalk, it makes her no more beautiful than your wife even if she is... and think I bet the poor guy spends about 95% of what should be his enjoyable leisure time worrying where she is what she is doing and who is thinking the same as you. so really his grass isn't any better than yours.

You know the same really applies to cars, houses, everything. I came down the motorway last night and passed a lorry, I was of course doing the legally allowed speed... wow I was going to get home faster than the poor chap. Half an hour later there he was right beside me. His grass was just the same as mine whether or not I stressed myself watching the mirrors for distant blue lights. Oh of course it is nice to have the material things in life but it doesn't make your neighbour better if he has one model up from you... he will get to the office just like you... probably more stressed because he has already started worrying what his wife is doing, if the car will get scratched in the carpark and how he will manage to keep up the payments as his wife has run all his credit cards to max. You see his grass actually isn't anything like as green as yours and him worrying about it is going to take years off his life. So, the next time you watch her walk down the road, walk back to your lawn and breathe a sigh of relief.

I do hope that at least some of my efforts have been enjoyable. I have enjoyed putting it together I will not deny. I am fortunate that I have an open stage on which to express myself. My books may or may not sell but I am happy with the effort I expend in doing it... my grass is as green as anybody's. Oh, and watch out there are more to come!

Something Completely Nuts
poems and ramblings

Chris Dyer
www.chrisdyerauthor.com

About the Author

Although I have always enjoyed writing my love for horses has been instrumental in most of my books, and my knowledge, which I class myself fortunate to have gathered, as it has helped me in my writing. It has also given me the opportunity to formulate natural remedies for horses. I have an association with an international equine products company. Who are very demanding in their requirements, of which I am glad, and I have produced several formulas that I hope they will market once trials are completed. I would say to all that I feel blessed as I am doing the things that I love to do. It is hard work and I have to say it hasn't always been like this… like everyone, there have been serious low points in my life, even to the point of living on a beach wondering where my next meal would come from. I hope as you read this you will have determination and "never say die". Whatever you are doing or wish to do keep at it, there is a strong possibility that if you are determined enough it will come through for you in the end.

Titles from Chris Dyer

The Beginning: Book One The Sapphire Staff
Plants Potions and Oils For Horses, J.A. Allen (Crowood Press)

The Rocket Series:
Sting in the Tail
From Rocket with Love
Storm Brewing
(Monday Creek Publishing 2017)

Something Completely Different: Poems, Proverbs, Rhymes
Something Completely Weird: Poems, Proverbs and Stuff
Something Completely Odd: Poems and Ramblings
Something Completely Crazy: More Poems and Ramblings
Something Completely Insane: Even More Poems and Ramblings
Something Completely Nuts: Poems and Ramblings
(Monday Creek Publishing 2017)

www.ingramcontent.com/pod-product-compliance
Lightning Source LLC
Chambersburg PA
CBHW071421040426
42445CB00012BA/1242